When Bad Dogs Happen to Good People!

When Bad Dogs Happen to Good People!

LAUREL WRIGHT AND GEORGE MORAN

Crown Publishers, Inc.
NEW YORK

Published by Crown Publishers, Inc., One Park Avenue,
New York, New York 10016 and simultaneously
in Canada by General Publishing Company Limited

Manufactured in the United States of America

Library of Congress Cataloging in Publication Data

Wright, Laurel.
  When bad dogs happen to good people!

  1. Dogs—Anecdotes, facetiae, satire, etc.
2. Dogs—Caricatures and cartoons.   3. American wit
and humor, Pictorial.   I. Moran, George, 1942–
II. Title.
PN6231.D68W74   1983   741.5'973   83-7625
ISBN 0-517-55133-0

10 9 8 7 6 5 4 3 2 1

First Edition

For Bonky . . .

who bit Garp

Introduction

There is only one question that truly matters: Why do bad dogs happen to good people? Yesterday, a young boy came to my office and poured out his soul.

"When my dad brought home the collie I thought he would be my best friend and fetch sticks and save me from close calls, just like Lassie on TV. Instead he lies under the couch all day shedding and pooping, and when I take him for a walk he knocks over every garbage can on the Grand Concourse, and he bit Aunt Myra's finger off. Why, Rabbi Schnauzer? I'm a nice boy. Why did this bad dog have to happen to me?"

The truth is, bad dogs are visited upon the strong and the weak, the good and the bad, the just and the unjust. Bad dogs track muddy paw prints on the marble floors of princes and on the cracked linoleum of clerks. Like Cerberus at the gates of hell, bad dogs howl at the gilded doors of the rich and the tenement doors of the poor. Cowardly collies, sociopathic mutts, perverted Dobermans: bad dogs come in all sizes, shapes, and breeds. Executives, chimney sweeps, Valley girls: bad dogs inflict pain and hardship on people in all walks of life. No one is immune to the canine blight.

I, too, have suffered the fate of a bad dog. It was a squawking, gluttonous little Pomeranian left to me by a distant relation. Huey (for such was the creature's name) chewed up my heirloom Torah, consumed the family's T-bone steak—with milk—and ate the baby. It just didn't seem fair. Weren't we good people? Why had God sent us such a bad dog?

I do not know why bad dogs happen to good people. I only know that sometimes they do. Bad dogs are a law of nature, a fact of life, and just one of those things.

Bad dogs simply are.

RABBI BEN SCHNAUZER

When Bad Dogs Happen to Good People!

ONE DAY AT THE VET'S

Bad Doggerel

"Every dog shall have his day,"
a phrase I've heard a lot.
But what will happen when the day arrives
for Fido, Snoopy, Spot?

Will we have to learn to walk on fours
and dress in dog disguise?
Will we have to chew on shoes and bones?
Will it rain cats and guys?

Will all the dogs in all the world
unite in one loud bark
and join each other in a trotting march
to a canines-only ark?

And watch with glee while the land fills up
with a flood they knew would come
and watch while all their masters drown—
gosh, it makes me glum.

To think how I carefully feed that dog
and brush his coat and tail!
So what if I keep him on a leash
and once left him out in the hail.

I love my dog; my dog loves me,
but that won't mean a lot
when the dog rains come and the day arrives
for Fido, Snoopy, Spot.

The Savage Afghan and the Hapless Housekeeper

Wasn't it enough that each day Nell Smith dutifully commuted from Flushing to care for the exclusive Tudor home of her wealthy Westchester employers? Did she also have to endure the ill will of their equally exclusive Afghan hound?

Yes, she did.

And no, there is no explaining why. . . .

The Suicidal Poodle and the Fashion Editor

Suicide, you might well believe, is the private act of a desperate individual. Maybe so. And yet a fashion editor of my acquaintance would disagree.

"Ever since I brought Fifi to my offices at *Dazzle* magazine, she has tyrannized me with her endless attempts at self-slaughter. Whenever I am faced with a deadline or late for a show of the spring collections, she forces me to save her miserable life. What have I done to deserve this horrible little dog?"

Again, the unanswerable question, this time from a woman whose only sin was to acquire a dog that would coordinate well with her accessories. . . .

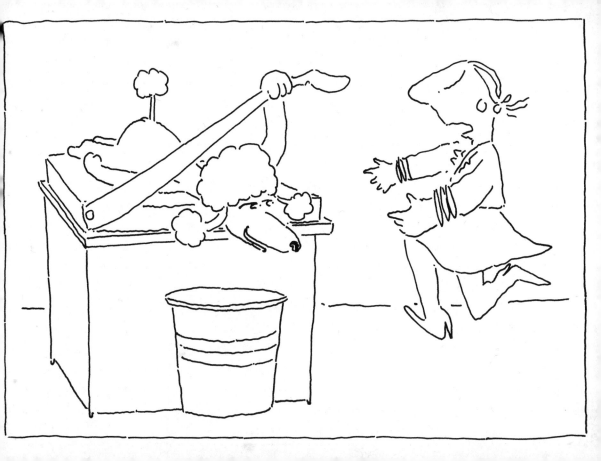

More Bad Doggerel

Oh, keep the dog far hence, far hence
is what the poet wrote.
Oh, keep the dog beyond the door,
the path, the gate, the moat.
Oh, keep the dog away from the house
and far from the car and boat.
And think twice before you let the dog
inside your canvas tote.

The Dastardly Dalmatian and Engine Company 39

A litter of eight Dalmatians and which did Captain Spaniel Field choose for his firehouse but the one pup destined for dastardly doghood—proof positive that this is a chancy universe at best, and that God, and fire chiefs, play dice. . . .

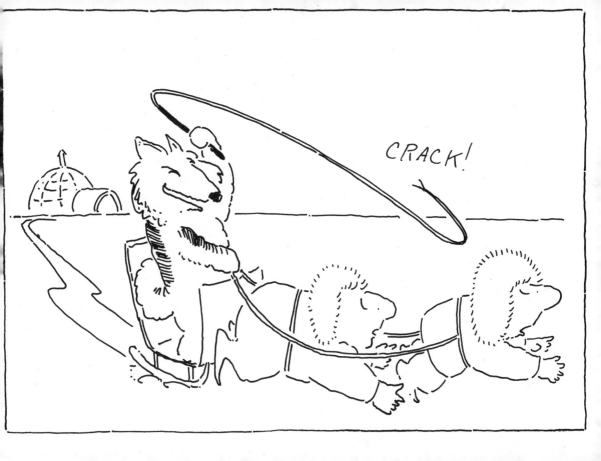

The Numberless Yorkies and the Valley Girl

Some said it was her love of worldly goods that sealed her fate.

Others said it was her false idols (to her, God was an awesome dude in homeroom).

But the tragedy of the Valley girl and the numberless Yorkies required the preexistence of only two things: shag rugs and a hoard of bad dogs diabolical enough to disguise themselves as such.

One cannot make sense of these things. Sometimes there just is no explanation.

Yet More Bad Doggerel

No doubt your mind is in a fog
when it comes to naming your dastardly dog.
Names like Champ and Sport won't do,
but names like these are fitting and true:

Name it Bummer; name it Gore;
name it Herpes, Pox, or Bore.
Try out Hairbag; call it Peeve,
Bane, Benito, Pigbrain, Skeeve,
Onan, Manson, Greaseball, Irk,
Kinky, Killjoy, Feeb, or Jerk.

Name it Stinko, Cooty, Snot,
Barfy, Blunder, Bonehead, Rot.
Call it Smegma, Mucus, Fester;
call it Crotch or Wretch or Pester.
Churl's a good name. So is Nero.
So is Scrooge and Scourge and Zero.
Call it Earthscum; call it Sod;
Call it Ratso, Ringworm, Clod.

I named my bad dog Wrath o' God.

The Parasite-Chihuahua and the Quarterback

"Bad dogs simply are." I wrote the words myself, yet when I think upon the case of the Dallas quarterback and the Chihuahua I am struck by how little they could possibly console this unfortunate athlete.

These are the sad facts:

Our quarterback, an exemplary citizen, was visiting an elderly neighbor when her pet Chihuahua began to have puppies. When he bent down to take a closer look, one of the tiny, mouselike creatures became attached to the athlete in the process that men of science call imprinting. The pup affixed itself to our hero's face, never to release its tenacious grip.

Our quarterback was faced with a difficult moral choice. Should he have the creature surgically removed, causing it physical and mental trauma, or should he accept what fate had accorded him? With great courage, he took the latter course.

"I know I don't deserve this hardship," he mumbles from behind the creature's belly, "but what will be will be. The Chihuahua cleaves unto me and I shall cleave unto the Chihuahua."

Despite his terrible affliction, the quarterback bravely resumed his career—an inspiration to any victim of a bad dog.

Enough Already with the Bad Doggerel

My dog's meaner than your dog.
My dog growls in his sleep,
chewing on leftover human bones,
counting mutilated sheep.

My dog's meaner than your dog.
My dog prowls all night,
sniffing for whiffs of baby's blood
to use in a sinister rite.

He sets out stones in a circle.
Inside, he piles the bones.

He wheezes and spits out baby's blood,
and all the world groans.

My dog's meaner than your dog.
My dog howls all day.
My dog's got no conscience at all.
Y'all better pray

that my dog doesn't find you.
Cause, baby, if he do,
he's gonna gouge your eyes out
and get your mama, too.

About the Authors

LAUREL WRIGHT is the pseudonymous alter ego of a generally solemn poet and essayist whose work has appeared in publications ranging from *Glamour* magazine to *The Little Magazine*. She identifies strongly with the suicidal poodle and is up for the coveted Chutzpa Prize for her impersonation of Ben Schnauzer, the world's only shiksa rabbi.

GEORGE MORAN, our illustrator, is the coauthor with Jim Erskine of *Throw a Tomato, Fold a Banana, Hug a Teddy,* and *Lie Down and Roll Over* and is the author/creator of *Eggs*. He has never forgotten the Christmas of 1961 when Rufus, his willful basset hound, in an orgy of triumph and gluttony, dragged the family's seventeen-pound turkey down the dining-room table to the sound of gasps and shattering crystal.